Alfresco Cuisine

Andrew and Hazel Armstrong

For Cooks On The Move

First published 1996
by The British Horse Society
British Equestrian Centre
Stoneleigh Park,
Kenilworth, Warwickshire
CV8 2LR
Tel: 01203 696697 Fax: 01203 690426

A catalogue record of this book is available from the British Library

ISBN 1 901292 00 2

Produced by: Beckett Karlson Ltd
Westminster House
Ermine Business Park
Huntingdon
Cambs PE18 6XY
Tel: 01480 435509 Fax: 01480 413178

Distributed jointly by: The British Horse Society and Beckett Karlson Ltd

DEDICATION

The authors wish to dedicate this book to Hubert Reynolds, who retired as Director of the Access & Rights of Way Department in 1996. During his six years with the Society, Hubert, known to love both good food and fine wines, encouraged and supported both his staff and volunteers in achieving things that they had hitherto thought impossible. His drive, determination and dedication to this cause knew no bounds and many people have much to thank him for. Hubert joined the Department as Project Officer for Access & Riding Rights of Way and it was through his vision that the '..... on Horseback' trail guides were born. He is wished a long and happy retirement with time to enjoy both preparing and eating the recipes from this book.

ACKNOWLEDGEMENTS

A number of people have given their time and expertise to provide details for this book which has been produced in celebration of the British Horse Society's Golden Jubilee. The profits from the sale of this book will go towards the Access & Rights of Way Department's work in protecting our heritage of riding routes.

In particular thanks are given to Steve Davies and Paul Holness of Beckett Karlson for their help with production and funding of this project; Sarah Bailey for the cartoon drawings of 'Mr Al Fresco'; Sue Pilcher and Sheila Hardy of the Access & Rights of Way Department for their commitment to this unusual project and for giving their time so readily to produce and proof-read the copy.

But most of all thanks are due to Hazel Armstrong, County Bridleways Officer for Humberside, and her husband Andrew, who have begged or borrowed all these recipes from their friends, then tried and tested them in order to produce this book which it is hoped will become an invaluable companion to all who enjoy a life out of doors.

Please note: These recipes have been collected over a number of years and from many different sources and you will undoubtedly recognise some variations of one or two of your own family favourites which have been 'doctored' as they have changed hands. It is not the authors intention to claim them as originals!

THE BRITISH HORSE SOCIETY

(Registered Charity No. 210504)

The British Horse Society is a national charity and was founded in 1947 when two separate equestrian bodies - The National Horse Association and the Institute of the Horse and Pony Club - decided to join forces and work together for the good of both horse and rider. It is a marriage that has proved to be a great success and the British Horse Society has steadily increased its membership from just 4000 in the late 1960's to over 65,000 as it celebrates its Golden Jubilee in 1997.

By becoming members of the British Horse Society, horse lovers know they are joining a body of people with a shared interest in the horse. Members can be sure that they are contributing to the work of the leading equine charity with a primary aim to improve the standards of care for horses and ponies. Welfare is not only about the rescuing of horses in distress (which we do); it is also about acting to prevent abuse in the first place. There are many means to achieving this: by teaching and advising, by looking to the horse's well-being and safety, by providing off-road riding, by encouraging high standards in all equestrian establishments, and fighting for the horse's case with government and in Europe.

The British Horse Society works tirelessly towards these aims thanks to the work of its officials at Stoneleigh in its specialist departments and its army of dedicated volunteers out in the field. The principle aim of the Access & Rights of Way Department is to make the countryside more accessible to riders and to campaign on their behalf. The volunteers based on county networks, monitor access to the countryside and work to open up and protect bridleways and byways in each county, often involving a long drawn-out legal process, in order to make riding and driving safer, by taking horse and rider off busy roads. To this end, the department publishes many free leaflets covering all aspects of access and rights of way.

The Access & Riding Rights of Way (ARROW) Project was embarked upon in 1990 and has meant that over 5000 kilometres of bridleway have been identified and published as part of a series of trail guides with more to follow. These '... on Horseback' guide books covering various regions of the UK, give easy to follow instructions to circular and linear trails using byways, bridleways and quiet country roads as links. They include information about accommodation for both horse and rider, hints on riding the trails, valuable advice on safety aspects and a code of practice for riding responsibly. They are equally suitable for walkers and cyclists. Some are designed for carriage drivers.

Membership benefits the horse lover as well as the horse; the Society can offer something to all equestrians, whether they are weekend riders, interested spectators or keen competitors. The benefits include free Third Party Public Liability and Personal Accident Insurance, free legal advice, free publications, reductions to British Horse Society events, special facilities at the major shows, and free advice and information on any equine query.

Largely financed by its membership subscriptions, the Society welcomes the support of all horse lovers. If you are thinking of joining the Society and would like to find out more about our work, please contact the Membership Department at the British Horse Society, British Equestrian Centre, Stoneleigh Park, Kenilworth, Warwickshire, CV8 2LR. Telephone: 01203 696697

Contents

1

One or Two Ring Cooking

Bacon Pancakes
Cheese and Onions
Cheesey Potato Fritters
Mango Chicken
Chicken and Banana Curry
Curried Rice
Elegant Pork
Corned Beef Feeding A Crowd
Fusilli with Chicken and Tomatoes
Leeks and Bacon
Mussels in Tomato Sauce
Poverty Sausage Patties
Porcupine Balls
Prawn and Egg Curry
Quick Macaroni Cheese
Sausage and Bacon with Noodles
Saucy Liver
Sweet and Sour Salmon
Tuna Macaroni
Vegetable Curry
Warm Bean and Tuna Salad
West Indian Risotto

Hi! I'm Al Fresco, look out for my tips.

Bacon Pancake

1 lge		Potato
4oz	(113g)	Bacon rashers
1 small		Onion
1		Egg
1oz	(28g)	Plain flour
		Worcestershire sauce
		Oil
		Salt and pepper

1. Remove the bacon rinds and chop bacon into small pieces.

2. Coarsely grate the potato and onion.

3. Mix all the ingredients together.

4. Heat a little oil in a frying pan. Pour in the mixture and cook for 7 minutes on each side.

   2 good portions - serves 2/3.

Cheese And Onions

2 lge	Onions, sliced
8oz (225g)	Strong cheese, grated
1 tblspn	Oil
1 dessertspoon	Cornflour
1 dessertspoon	Burdalls gravy salt
¾ pt (425ml)	Water

1. Make a gravy with the gravy salt, cornflour and water.

2. Fry the onions in a saucepan until browned.

3. Pour the gravy over the onions, and bring to the boil stirring well.

4. Remove from the heat and stir in the cheese until it has melted.

Serves 2/3.

Cheesy Potato Fritters

6oz	(150g)	Can condensed tomato soup
4oz	(113g)	Cheese, grated
4		Eggs
½ pint mug		Left over mashed potato
4 level tblspns		Self Raising flour
1oz	(28g)	Butter or margarine

1. Beat all of the ingredients together with a fork.

2. Heat a little margarine or butter in a frying pan and fry small spoonsful of the mixture on both sides until golden brown.

3. Serve hot.

Serves 4.

Mango Chicken

4		Boneless chicken breasts
6oz	(170g)	Mango chutney
½ pt	(250ml)	Chicken stock (or water and a stock cube)
1oz	(28g)	Butter
1 tspn		Curry powder
		Freshly ground black pepper

1. Melt the butter in a saucepan, add the chicken and fry until golden.

2. Add the mango chutney, curry powder and pepper to taste.

3. Add the chicken stock (or water and stock cube).

4. Bring to the boil then cover and simmer until cooked and the sauce has thickened.

Serves 4.

Chicken & Banana Curry

4	Chicken Pieces
1	Onion
1 pt (560ml)	Chicken Stock (or water and 2 chicken stock cubes)
2 tblspns	Vegetable Oil
2 tblspns	Curry Paste
1	Lemon grated zest and juice
2	Bananas
	Salt and pepper
	Creamed coconut (optional)
	Fresh chillies (optional)

1. In a large saucepan fry the onion and chicken until golden brown.

2. Mix in the curry paste, mashed bananas, creamed coconut, and the lemon juice and zest.

3. Add the chicken stock (or water and stock cubes) and bring to the boil then reduce the heat and simmer for 45 minutes.

4. Adjust seasoning. (If you prefer a hotter curry the fresh chillies can be added.)

Serves 4.

Curried Rice

1		Onion, chopped
6oz	(170g)	Long grain rice
1 pt	(560ml)	Water
1		Chicken stock cube
		Pinch turmeric
1 level tspn		Curry powder
		Salt and freshly ground black pepper
		Butter
		Parsley, chopped

1. Melt the butter, add the onions and fry until soft.

2. Add the rice and cook for 2 minutes.

3. Add the water, stock cube and seasonings and simmer gently until all the stock has been absorbed.

4. Allow to cool. Sprinkle with chopped parsley before serving.

Serves 2 as main dish, 3 as a side dish.

Elegant Pork

2 lbs (908g)	Lean pork, cut into 1" cubes
10oz (283g)	Sliced mushrooms
1 pkt	Onion soup
1 tbspn	Plain flour
1	Clove garlic, crushed
2oz (56g)	Butter or margarine
2 cups	Water
1 cup	Red wine
Handful	Chopped parsley

1. Melt the butter in a large frying pan, add the pork and garlic, cook until the meat is browned and tender.
2. Remove from the pan.
3. Add the flour and dry onion soup and mix into the fat remaining in the pan.
4. Gradually add the water and red wine.
5. Simmer uncovered for 10 minutes, stirring occasionally.
6. Add the meat, mushrooms and chopped parsley, heat through (5 mins approx).
7. Serve over noodles or boiled rice.

Serves 4/6.

Corned Beef Feeding A Crowd

2 cups	Long grain rice		Worcester sauce
1	Onion, finely chopped		White pepper
2	Cloves garlic, crushed	4-8oz	Mushrooms. sliced
14oz (400g)	Tin chopped tomatoes	1	Pepper, diced (any colour)
2	Beef stock cubes	1 cup	Frozen or fresh garden peas
1oz	Butter	1 tin	Corned beef, diced small
1 dessertspoon	Dried oregano	4-6oz	Cheese, grated
	Water (1 tomato can)		

(If you prefer, or you do not have any corned beef you can substitute 4 chopped Chorizo or similar spicy smoked sausage).

1. Melt the butter in a large pan. Fry the onions and garlic until soft.

2. Add all the vegetables except peas and fry for 2-3 minutes.

3. Add the rice, tomatoes, water and oregano.

4. Crumble 2 beef stock cubes into the mixture and add worcester sauce to taste.
5. Bring to the boil, cover and simmer until the rice is cooked and nearly all the liquid is absorbed.

6. Add the peas, corned beef or sausages and heat through.

7. Serve very hot onto plates and sprinkle with plenty of grated cheese.

Serves 4/6.

Fusilli With Chicken And Tomatoes

12oz	(340g)	Fusilli
14oz	(400g)	Tin chopped tomatoes
8oz	(225g)	Cooked shredded chicken
4oz	(113g)	Diced mozzarella cheese
3 tblspns		Olive oil
1 tspn		Sugar
1 tblspn		Parmesan cheese
1 tblspn		Tomato puree
½ tspn		Dried oregano
		Salt and pepper

1. Cook the pasta in boiling water for 15-20 minutes then drain.

2. Place all the ingredients except the chicken and cheese into a large saucepan. Stir and bring to the boil, then simmer for 15 minutes.

3. Add the chicken and cook for a further 5 minutes

4. Reduce the heat, mix in the pasta and mozzarella cheese and stir until the cheese has melted.

5. Serve onto plates and sprinkle with grated parmesan cheese.

Serves 4.

Leeks And Bacon

8oz	(225g)	Smoked bacon
2 lge		Leeks (whites and green) cleaned and sliced
1oz	(28g)	Dripping for frying

1. Steam the leeks, drain well and keep warm.
2. Fry the bacon in the dripping until well browned.
3. Add the leeks and season with white pepper and salt.
4. Fry the leeks until they start to brown.
5. Serve with chunks of crusty bread.

Serves 4.

Mussels In Tomato Sauce

2 lb	(900g)	Fresh mussels
10.6oz	(300g)	Can condensed cream of tomato soup
1		Onion, finely chopped
2		Cloves garlic, crushed
2 tblspns		Chopped parsley
5 tblspns		White wine
		Salt and freshly ground black pepper

1. Scrub the mussels well, remove all the beard (stringy part attached to the shell) and set aside the cleaned mussels.

2. Put the remaining ingredients into a large pan and bring to the boil. Simmer for 3 minutes.

3. Add the mussels and bring back to the boil and simme for 10 minutes or until the mussels have opened well.

4. Discard any mussels which have not opened.

5. Serve piping hot in soup bowls garnished with parsley.

Serves 4.

Poverty Sausage Patties

8oz	(227g)	Potatoes, peeled and grated
8oz	(227g)	Pork sausage meat
1 small		Onion, grated
1		Apple, peeled and grated
1		Egg, beaten
		Salt and pepper

1. Drain any excess moisture from the potatoes.
2. Mix in the remaining ingredients.
3. Fry in small spoonsful in shallow fat until brown (about 7-8 minutes a side), turning during cooking.

Serves 4.

Porcupine Balls

1 lb	(454g)	Minced beef
2oz	(56g)	Uncooked rice
1 med		Onion, chopped
1 tspn		Salt
1		Beaten egg
1 can		Condensed tomato soup
2		Gloves garlic, crushed
1oz		Lard or dripping

1. Mix the mince, rice, salt, onion and beaten egg with 4 tblspns of the condensed tomato soup.

2. Wet your hands, divide and form the mixture into 12-16 balls.

3. Melt the fat in a saucepan and fry the garlic until golden brown.

4. Add the meatballs and fry until browned all over, then drain any excess fat.

5. Add the remaining soup and 1 can of water and bring to the boil,stirring occasionally.

6. Reduce the heat, cover and simmer for 40 minutes.

Serves 4.

Prawn And Egg Curry

8oz	(225g)	Frozen prawns, thawed
10.4oz	(295g)	Condensed asparagus soup
1		Onion, finely chopped
1		Clove garlic, crushed
½ tspn		Curry powder
4		Hard boiled eggs, shelled and halved
		Juice of ½ lemon
1 tblspn		Oil

1. Heat the oil in a pan and saute the onions, garlic and curry powder for 5 minutes on a low heat.

2. Add the prawns and soup and stir well.

3. Finally add the lemon juice and eggs. Heat through and serve with long grain and wild rice.

Serves 2/3.

Quick Macaroni Cheese

6oz	(170g)	Cooked macaroni
4		Rashers smoked bacon
2 small		Onion, chopped
1 can		Chicken soup
½ can		Milk
4oz	(113g)	Strong cheese, grated
1oz	(28g)	Lard or dripping

1. In a large frying pan fry the bacon and onions until light brown.

2. Stir in the soup, milk and 3oz (85g) of the cheese (*). Stir until smooth.

3. Add the macaroni.

4. Put the mixture into an ovenproof dish and sprinkle with the remaining cheese.

5. Place under a hot grill until the top is golden brown.

(*) IF A GRILL IS NOT AVAILABLE ALL OF THE CHEESE MAY BE ADDED AT STAGE 2

Sausages And Bacon With Noodles

12		Thin cut streaky bacon rashers de-rinded & diced	1	Red pepper, deseeded and chopped
1 lb	(454g)	Sausages	1	Clove garlic, crushed
1oz	(28g)	Margarine or butter	½ tspn	Sugar
16oz	(454g)	Can chopped tomatoes		Salt and pepper
12oz	(350g)	Noodles	1 lge	Onion, chopped
2 tblspns		Tomato puree	2-3	Sprigs fresh parsley
1 tblspn		Oil		

1. Melt the margarine or butter and oil and saute the garlic, onions and diced bacon for 5 minutes until soft.
2. Add the pepper, tomatoes and tomato puree.
3. Bring to the boil and simmer gently for about 10 minutes until the sauce is thick.
4. Season and add the sugar.
5. Fry the sausages or BBQ for about 10 minutes each side.
6. Cook the noodles in plenty of boiling salted water for about 12-15 minutes until just tender. Drain well and arrange on a flat dish.
7. Spoon the tomato mixture down the centre and arrange the sausages on top.

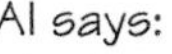

Serves 4/6.

Saucy Liver

1 lb	(454g)	Lambs' liver
15oz	(425g)	Can cream of mushroom soup
8oz	(225g)	Cooking apples, peeled cored and chopped
4oz	(100g)	Streaky bacon, rind removed and chopped
2 med		Onions, sliced
1		Clove garlic, chopped (optional)
¼ level tspn		Dried mixed herbs
		Salt & pepper to taste

1. Heat the oil in a frying pan and fry the onions, garlic and liver until lightly browned on all sides.

2. Add the bacon and apples and cook for 5 minutes.

3. Stir in the soup, seasoning and herbs. Cover and cook for 15-20 minutes, stirring occasionally, until liver is tender.

Serves 4.

Sweet And Sour Salmon

4	Salmon fillets
1 jar	Sweet and sour sauce
1 med can	Pineapple chunks
12oz (340g)	Egg noodles
2 tblspns	Olive oil
4	Spring onions, chopped

1. Saute the salmon in the oil (5 mins).
2. Add the sweet and sour sauce, simmer for about 2 minutes.
3. Add the pineapple chunks and spring onions and heat through.
4. Serve on a bed of noodles.

Serves 4.

Tuna Macaroni

12oz (340g)	Macaroni
1 can	Condensed mushroom soup
1 can (250g)	Tuna, drained and flaked
	Sliced tomatoes (to garnish)
2-3	Sprigs fresh parsley

1. Cook macaroni in boiling salted water until just tender and drain then return to the pan.

2. Add the flaked tuna.

3. Add the soup straight from the tin and heat gently.

4. When heated through serve onto plates and top with the sliced tomatoes and fresh parsley.

Serves 4/6.

Vegetable Curry

1	Courgette, diced	2 tspns	Garam masala
1	Medium potato, roughly diced	1 tspn	Fresh ginger, chopped
½	Cauliflower, broken into florets	4oz (113g)	Mushrooms, sliced
1	Onion, chopped	1 lge tin	Chopped tomatoes
1	Carrot, sliced	1 small tin	Baked beans
2	Cloves garlic, crushed	1 tblspn	Oil
½ pt	(280ml) Vegetable stock (or water and a stock cube)	3 tblspns	Curry paste

1. Fry the onion and garlic in a large saucepan until soft.

2. Add the ginger and curry paste and cook for 1 minute.

3. Add all the vegetables, tomatoes, baked beans and stock.

4. Bring to the boil, then reduce the heat and simmer for 20-25 minutes.

5. Add the Garam Masala, stir and serve.

Serves 4.

Warm Bean And Tuna Salad

2 x 14oz	(400g)	Tinned cannellini beans
8oz	(250g)	Tin tuna, drained and flaked
¼ pt	(142ml)	Olive oil
		Juice of ½ lemon
1 small		Red onion, thinly sliced
2-3		Sprigs fresh parsley

1. Heat the beans in their own juice in a pan then drain.

2. Warm the olive oil and lemon juice together.

3. Toss the beans in the olive oil and lemon juice mixture.

4. Make a ring of warm beans on a dish.

5. Place the flaked tuna in the centre of the beans and scatter the sliced onions over the top.

6. Garnish with fresh parsley.

Serves 4.

West Indian Rissotto

6oz	(185g)	Cooked long grain rice	1 Onion, finely chopped
5½oz	(156g)	Can condensed cream of celery soup	1 Clove garlic, crushed
			2 Bananas, peeled and sliced
6oz	(185g)	Peeled prawns	Juice of 1 lime
1 small		Red pepper, cored and finely chopped	Salt and pepper
			Flaked coconut
1 tblspn		Oil	
1 tspn		Chilli sauce (more if you wish)	

1. Heat the oil in a pan. Add the onion and garlic and fry for 5 minutes.

2. Add the remaining ingredients (except coconut) and mix well.

3. Cook over a low heat for 5 minutes.

4. Garnish with flaked coconut and serve.

   Serves 4.

2

Don't Wait By The Hob, Get On With A Job

(These recipes need a minimum of attention and take from 20 minutes to 1½ hours to cook).

Bean Pie
Bobotie
Cheesey Bacon Bake
Cheese Batter Pudding
Cheesey Leeks
Cheesey Tomato and Mushroom Layer Bake
Chicken Cacciatore
Chicken Divan
Devilled Pork
Ham and Leek Rolls
Maggies Mince
Ocean Pie
Pork Chops in Ginger Ale
Quick Cassoulet
Chicken Casserole
Quick Fish in Sauce
Rice and Chicken Pudding
Salmon Savoury
Stuffed Rolled Haddock
Steak Upside-Down Pie
Tomato Pudding
Travellers Pie

Bean Pie

1 tin		Baked beans
½ dessertspoon		Dried mustard
2oz		Cheddar cheese, grated
3oz	(80g)	White bread crumbs
1½ lb	(680g)	Cooked mashed potato

1. Place the beans into a pie dish.

2. Cover with the bread crumbs and sprinkle on the dried mustard.

3. Cover with grated cheese, then with a thick layer of mashed potato.

4. Bake at gas mark 4/180C/350F for 45 minutes or until nicely browned.

Serves 4.

Al says:
If there appears to be a lot of juice in the bean tin, drain a drop off before use. For a change add 2 teaspoons of curry powder to the beans or a scattering of your favourite herb.

Bobotie

1½ lb	(1.13kg)	Lean minced lamb or beef	2 tblspns	Olive oil
14oz	(440g)	Tin chopped tomatoes	2 tblspns	Tomato puree
2oz	(56g)	Flaked almonds	1 tblspn	Curry paste
3oz	(85g)	No soak apricots, sliced	1	Onion, chopped
½ pt	(285ml)	Lamb stock (or water and a stock cube)	1	Clove garlic, crushed
			2	Eggs
½ pt	(285ml)	Double cream		Seasoning to taste

1. Fry the mince in a large saucepan until brown. Remove from the pan.
2. Fry the onions and garlic until lightly browned.
3. Add the curry paste and cook for 1 minute.
4. Add the stock, tomatoes, tomato puree, seasoning, apricots and almonds.
5. Return the lamb to the pan, and bring to the boil then reduce the heat and simmer gently.
6. Lightly grease an ovenproof dish.
7. Spoon the mince into the dish.
8. Mix the cream and eggs together and pour over the mince.
9. Bake for 35 minutes gas mark 5/375F/190C until the top is set and golden.
10. Leave to rest for 5 minutes before serving.

Serves 4/6.

Cheesey Bacon Bake

1 lb	(454g)	Lean bacon
8oz	(225g)	Grated cheese
1 lge can		Tomatoes
1oz	(28g)	White bread crumbs
		Salt and pepper

1. Cut bacon into small pieces and fry until lightly browned. Place in a casserole dish.

2. Pour tomatoes over the bacon.

3. Mix the cheese and bread crumbs and sprinkle over the tomatoes.

4. Bake for 20 minutes gas mark 4/350F/180C.

Serves 2/4.

Cheese Batter Pudding

6oz	(170g)	Flour
1 pt	(570ml)	Milk
2		Eggs
½ lb	(225g)	Strong cheese
		Oil or lard to fry

1. Make a batter of the milk, eggs and flour. Leave to stand for 1 hour.

2. Grate the cheese and add half of it to the batter.

3. Heat oil or lard in Yorkshire Pudding tin until smoking.

4. Pour in batter.

5. Bake at gas mark 7/425F/220C for 25/30 mins until risen and lightly browned.

6. Sprinkle over the rest of the cheese, return to the oven until the cheese is crisply browned.

7. Can be served on its own or as a giant pudding with cheese and onions in chapter 1 of this book.

Serves 2/6

Cheesey Leeks

1 lb	(454g)	Chopped leeks
1 can		Condensed chicken or mushroom soup
8oz	(225g)	Strong grated cheese
4		Hard boiled eggs, sliced

1. Blanch the leeks in boiling water. Drain and keep warm, retain a small amount of the cooking liquid.

2. Warm the soup and stir in the cheese and the retained leek water.

3. Put the leeks in an ovenproof dish.

4. Arrange the sliced boiled eggs on top of the leeks.

5. Top with the cheesey sauce.

6. Bake for 20 minutes at gas mark 4/350F/180C.

Serves 4.

Cheesey Tomato and Mushroom Layer Bake

8oz	(225g)	Chopped mushrooms	2 Eggs
8oz	(225g)	Grated cheddar cheese	Black pepper
4oz	(113g)	Wholegrain rice	Fresh parsley
2 med		Chopped onions	
4 med		Tomatoes, thinly sliced	
2 tblspns		Oil	
1 dessertspoon		Bovril or Marmite	

1. Cook the rice in boiling water until tender and drain.
2. In a large saucepan fry the onion in the oil until tender.
3. Add the mushrooms and cook until soft.
4. Remove from the heat and stir in the cheese, Bovril or Marmite, egg, rice and pepper to taste.
5. Press half the mixture into a greased 2lb loaf tin and cover with half the sliced tomatoes.
6. Spoon in the remaining mixture and press down firmly.
7. Bake for 35 minutes, gas mark 5/375F/190C.
8. Allow to cool for a few minutes before turning out. Garnish with the remaining tomatoes and parsley.

Serves 4/6.

Chicken Cacciatore

4		Chicken joints
4oz	(113g)	Sliced button mushrooms
2oz	(56g)	Butter
1lb(454g)		Skinned fresh tomatoes
(or use 14oz (400g) tin chopped tomatoes)		
¼ pt	(142ml)	Chicken stock
(or use water and a stock cube)		

4 tblspns	Flour
1 tblspn	Olive Oil
1 level tspn	Salt
1 level tspn	Sugar
1 lge	Onion, chopped
1	Clove garlic, crushed
Pepper to taste	

1. Mix the flour, salt and pepper.

2. Toss the chicken pieces in the seasoned flour.

3. Heat the butter and oil in saucepan.

4. Fry the chicken joints until brown and crisp, remove from the pan.

5. Fry the onions and garlic in the butter and oil until pale gold.

6. Add the tomatoes, sugar and chicken stock.

7. Replace the chicken and bring slowly to the boil.

8. Cover and simmer for 45 minutes.

9. Add the mushrooms and simmer for a further 15-20 minutes.

Serves 4.

Chicken Divan

6	Chicken breasts
1 can	Heinz cream of chicken soup
1 cup	Grated cheese
1 tspn	Lemon juice
1 kilo	Frozen broccoli
1 cup	Mayonnaise
1 tspn	Curry powder

1. Blanche and drain the broccoli.

2. Place broccoli in a lasagne dish.

3. Place chicken breasts on top of the broccoli.

4. Mix all the remaining ingredients, except the cheese, and pour over the chicken.

5. Top with the grated cheese.

6. Do not cover. Bake for 1½ hours at gas mark 4/350F/180C. Do not over cook.

Serves 6.

Devilled Pork

4	Pork chops or slices	1 lge		Onion, chopped
2 tblspns	Vegetable oil	1 pt	(570ml)	Water
1 tblspn	Cornflour	2		Stock cubes
2 heaped tspns	Dried mustard	4		Cloves
2 tblspns	Tomato ketchup			Salt and pepper
2 tblspns	Brown sauce			

(an optional extra 10oz sliced mushrooms added to the casserole before baking and you'll have no pressing need for an extra vegetable.)

1. In a heavy frying pan brown the pork in the oil, remove and place in a casserole dish.
2. Fry the onion until soft. Add the flour and mustard and cook until slightly browned.
3. Add the water and then the rest of the ingredients (don't worry if it's a bit lumpy!) and stir well and bring slowly to the boil.
4. Pour sauce over the chops, and cover with a lid.
5. Bake for 45 minutes to 1 hour at gas mark 5/375F/190C.
6. Serve with baked jacket potatoes, which can be cooked at the same time.

Serves 4.

Ham and Leek Rolls

4		Leek whites steamed and drained
4		Slices of ham (prepacked will do)
1 can		Chicken, mushroom or celery soup
4oz	(113g)	Cheese, grated

1. Wrap a slice of ham around each leek.

2. Place in an ovenproof dish.

3. Pour the soup over the leeks and top with grated cheese.

4. Bake in the oven for ½ hour at gas mark 3/160C/325F.

Serves 2.

Maggies Mince

1 lb	(454g)	Minced beef
1 lge		Onion, finely chopped
1 tin		Oxtail soup
8oz	(227g)	Strong cheddar cheese, diced
		Salt & pepper
		Herbs to taste (optional)

1. Pre-heat the oven to gas mark 5-6/190-200C/375-400F.

2. Mix all the ingredients together.

3. Place in a pie dish.

4. Place in the centre of the oven and bake for 1 hour.

Serves 4.

Ocean Pie

1lb(454g)		White fish fillet	1 x 2oz	Jar crab spread
1lb(454g)		Potatoes	1 rounded tblspn	Plain flour
1oz	(28g)	Cheddar cheese		Milk
1oz	(28g)	Margarine		
½ lb	(227g)	Pack frozen mixed vegetables		

1. Half fill a large saucepan with water, add a heaped tspn of salt and bring to the boil.
2. Wash the fish, season with salt and pepper and place on a plate on top of pan of water. Cover and cook for 15-20 minutes depending on the thickness of the fish.
3. Wash, peel and slice the potatoes. Put them in the pan of boiling water under the plate of fish. Cook for 5-10 minutes until tender.
4. Cook the frozen mixed vegetables in boiling salted water following the directions on the packet.
5. Drain fish liquor from the plate into a measuring jug and make up to ½ pt. with milk.
6. Skin and flake fish, keep warm.
7. Melt the margarine in a saucepan, stir in the flour and cook gently for about 2 minutes without browning.
8. Add the liquor, bring to the boil, stirring continuously, simmer for 2 minutes.
9. Remove from the heat and add the crab meat paste, beat until smooth and season to taste.
10. Drain the mixed vegetables and add to the sauce together with the fish. Mix well and pour into a buttered 1½ pt (850ml) pie dish.
11. Prepare a hot grill. Drain the potatoes and arrange on the fish mixture. Top with grated cheese and grill until golden brown and bubbling.
12. Serve with crusty bread and butter.

Serves 4.

Pork Chops In Ginger Ale

4 or 5 lge	Pork chops
2oz (56g)	Butter
1 tblspn	Tomato puree
½ pt (284ml)	Ginger ale
2 lge	Onions, sliced
1 tspn	Brown sugar
1 tblspn	Plain flour
	Salt & pepper

1. Preset oven to gas mark 4/350F/180C.
2. Fry onions in a saute pan with ½ the butter until golden brown.
3. Remove the onions from the pan and place in an oven proof casserole.
4. Brown the chops on both sides in the remaining butter. Place chops on the onions in the casserole.
5. Sprinkle with the brown sugar.
6. Stir the flour into the butter remaining in the saute pan and cook to a golden brown.
7. Allow to cool slightly. Stir in the tomato puree and ginger ale.
8. Pour over the chops and season with salt and pepper.
9. Place in the oven and cook for 1 hour.

Serves 4.

QUICK CASSOULET

1 lb	(454g)	Tin haricot beans
1 lb	(454g)	Belly pork, cut into small cubes
1 lb	(454g)	Herb sausage, cut into small chunks
6		Small chicken breasts
10.6oz	(300g)	Condensed cream of tomato soup
10.6oz	(300g)	Condensed vegetable soup
1		Onion, chopped
2		Cloves garlic, crushed
6 tblspns		Fresh white bread crumbs

1. Preheat the oven, gas mark 3/325F/160C.
2. Put all the ingredients (except bread crumbs) into a large heavy casserole dish.
3. Stir gently then cover with water.
4. Cover the casserole and cook in the oven for 1 hour, (check the water level once during cooking).
5. Remove the lid and sprinkle the top with bread crumbs, put back in the oven and cook for a further 30 minutes. Serve straight from the pot.

Serves 6/8.

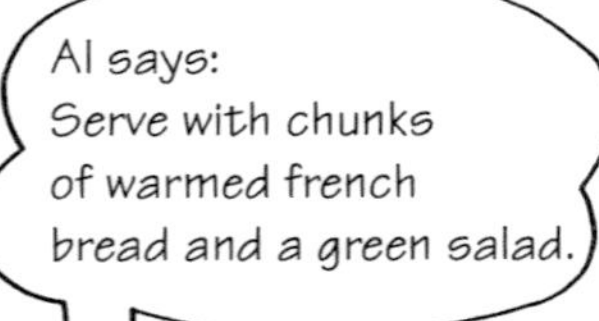

Chicken Casserole

4		Chicken joints
8		Button onions (or shallots)
10.6oz	(290g)	Can condensed mushroom soup
5 floz	(140ml)	Single cream
1		Red pepper, deseeded and chopped
¼ pt	(142ml)	Milk
1		Bay leaf
		Salt & pepper
1oz	(28g)	Butter

1. Melt the butter in a large saucepan, fry the chicken until golden brown.

2. Add the onions and red pepper and cook for 15 minutes.

3. Stir in the soup, milk and bay leaf.

4. Bring to the boil, cover and simmer for 45 minutes.

5. Stir in the cream salt and pepper to taste, remove the bay leaf and serve garnished with parsley.

   Serves 4.

Quick Fish in Sauce

2		Fillets skinned fish
1 can		Condensed mushroom soup
2oz	(56g)	Grated cheese

1. Place the fish in a shallow ovenproof dish.
2. Beat the soup in the can then spoon over the fish.
3. Top with the grated cheese.
4. Bake for 20 minutes at gas mark 6/400F/200C.
5. Serve with mashed potato.

Serves 2.

RICE & CHICKEN PUDDING

1 cup		Long grain rice	4oz	(113g)	Mushrooms, chopped
3oz	(85g)	Butter	8oz	(227g)	Cooked shredded chicken
2 lge		Onions, chopped	8oz	(227g)	Frozen flakey pastry
1 dessertspoon		Curry paste	2 cups		Chicken stock (or water and stock cube)

1. Melt 2oz butter in a heavy pan and fry ½ the onion until softened (2-3 minutes).
2. Add the rice and curry paste and cook gently for 2-3 minutes.
3. Add the stock, cook until the rice is tender and water absorbed.
4. Roll out ¾ of the pastry and line a 1 pint ovenproof pudding basin leaving plenty of overlap at the top.
5. Melt the remaining butter in a large pan and fry the remaining onions and the mushrooms until tender.
6. Remove from the heat and add the chicken and seasoning.
7. Mix in the cooked rice.
8. Place the mixture in the lined pudding basin.
9. Roll out the remaining pastry to cover the top, dampen the edges and seal.
10. Bake at gas mark 5/190C/375F for 45 minutes.
11. Invert and turn out onto an ovenproof serving plate and return to the oven for 15 minutes to brown the bottom.

Serves 4.

Salmon Savoury

1 can		Salmon
½ pt	(142ml)	Milk
1		Egg
2-3		Sprigs of parsley, chopped
2oz	(56g)	White bread crumbs
		Butter

1. Remove any skin and bones from the salmon and mash up well.

2. Whisk the egg and milk together.

3. Add the salmon and chopped parsley.

4. Place in a buttered ovenproof dish, sprinkle with the bread crumbs and dot with butter.

5. Bake for approx 15 minutes at gas mark 4/350F/180C until set and the top is golden brown.

Serves 2.

STUFFED HADDOCK ROLLS

2		Haddock fillets	1		Rasher streaky bacon
1		Egg	1oz	(25g)	Butter
1oz	(25g)	Grated cheddar cheese	1		Lemon
2 tspns		Parsley, chopped			Salt & pepper
2oz	(50g)	White bread crumbs			

1. Preheat the oven to gas mark 4/180C/350F
2. Hard boil the egg for 12 minutes, then shell and chop.
3. Mix together the egg, cheese, 1½ tspns chopped parsley and 1½ oz of bread crumbs.
4. Derind and chop the bacon,then fry until very lightly browned.
5. Add the bacon to the egg mixture.
6. Wash, skin and dry the haddock fillets.
7. Spread the egg mixture over the haddock fillets, then roll them starting from the tail end.
8. Place the rolled fillets into a buttered ovenproof dish, sprinkle with the remaining bread crumbs.
9. Place in the centre of the oven and bake for 20 minutes until golden brown.
10. Garnish with the remaining chopped parsley and lemon slices.

Serves 2.

Steak Upside - Down Pie

12oz	(340g)	Minced beef	6oz	(170g)	Self raising flour
¼ pt	(142ml)	Beef stock (or water and a stock cube)	2oz	(56g)	Butter
			2oz	(56g)	Cheddar cheese, grated
2-3		Tomatoes			
2oz	(56g)	Mushrooms, sliced	1		Egg yolk
2 med		Onions, chopped	1 tblspn		Milk
1oz	(28g)	Beef dripping			Salt & pepper

1. Melt the dripping in a saucepan and fry the minced beef until browned. Remove from the pan and keep warm.
2. Fry the vegetables until slightly browned.
3. Return the mince to the pan and add the stock.
4. Stir until it forms a smooth thick mixture.
5. Season well. Cook uncovered for 15 minutes, stirring from time to time.
6. Meanwhile sieve the flour with seasoning into a bowl.
7. Rub in the butter and grated cheese.
8. Bind together with the egg yolk and a little milk. Allow to rest in the fridge for 30 minutes.
9. Roll out to an 8 inch round.
10. Place the meat mixture into an ovenproof dish (a large souffle dish is ideal) and top with the pastry.
11. Bake for 50 minutes at gas mark 5/190C/375F in the centre of the oven.
12. To serve, invert onto a hot dish and accompany with buttered carrots and mashed potatoes.

Serves 4.

Tomato Pudding

2 x 14oz	(396g)	Tins chopped tomatoes
8oz	(227g)	Sliced gruyere cheese
1 pt	(568ml)	Milk
10		Slices white bread
2		Fresh tomatoes, sliced
2 tblspns		Fresh chopped parsley
1 tblspn		Dried basil
5		Eggs

1. Beat together the eggs and milk in a large bowl.
2. Dip the sliced bread in the egg mixture. Use some of the slices to cover the bottom of a greased 2.5 pint (1.5 ltr) oven proof dish.
3. Pour a third of the tinned tomatoes over the bread in the dish. Sprinkle with a few herbs and some of the cheese.
4. Continue to layer the dish with eggy bread and tomatoes finishing with cheese and herbs.
5. Top with the sliced tomatoes.
6. Bake for 40 minutes at gas mark 6/400F/200C.

Serves 4/6.

Traveller's Pie

4oz	(100g)	Cooked potatoes, sieved or riced	1 tspn	Baking powder
			4	Eggs
5oz	(125g)	Plain flour	1 tblspn	Parsley, chopped
3oz	(75g)	Butter		Salt and pepper
6oz	(150g)	Strong cheddar cheese, grated		

1. Cream the butter until soft.
2. Add the potatoes, flour, baking powder and salt. Blend well together.
3. Turn out onto a board and knead lightly.
4. Divide in two and roll out to about ¼ inch (0.5cm) thick rounds.
5. Place one of the rounds on a greased ovenproof plate and prick with a fork.
6. Sprinkle the cheese over the pastry, make four hollows in the cheese and break the eggs into these hollows.
7. Season with salt and pepper and sprinkle with parsley.
8. Cover with the second round of pastry, knock up the edges and flute with your fingers.
9. Brush with milk and make a slit in the centre.
10. Place in the oven and bake for 35 minutes at gas mark 6/400F/200C.
11. Serve with a green salad.

Serves 4.

Al says:
Your choice of herbs can be added to potato mixture.

3

"These Cook For A Bit Longer So Go For A Wander"

"These cook for a bit longer so go for a wander".

Baked Layered Vegetables

1 lb	(450g)	Potatoes, sliced
8oz	(225g)	Sliced carrots
4oz	(113g)	Green beans
2oz	(56g)	Sliced mushrooms
½		Cauliflower, broken into florets
½ pt	(280ml)	Milk
4oz	(113g)	Grated cheddar cheese
2		Eggs
		Salt & pepper

1. Layer all of the vegetables in a buttered casserole.
2. Cover with the grated cheese.
3. Beat the eggs and milk together, season and pour over the vegetables. Cover the dish.
4. Bake for 1½ hours gas mark 4/350F/180C until set and golden.

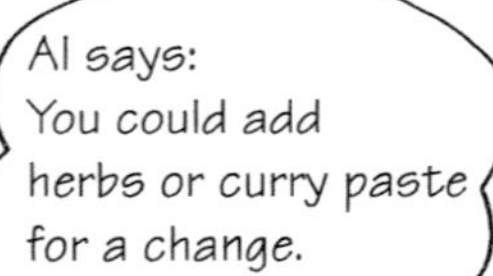

N.B. If there is a lot of juice from the vegetables, remove the lid for the last few minutes of cooking time to allow excess liquid to evaporate and the top to brown.

Serves 4.

"These cook for a bit longer so go for a wander".

BAKED LAYERED POTATOES

2 lb	(910g)	Potatoes, thinly sliced
6oz	(170g)	Grated cheddar cheese
1oz	(28g)	Butter
10 floz	(284ml)	Milk
1		Large sliced onion
		Salt & black pepper
		Fresh parsley

1. Layer the potatoes, onions, cheese and knobs of butter in a casserole, finishing with a layer of cheese.

2. Lightly season the milk and pour over the vegetables.

3. Bake for 1½ hours at gas mark 5/375F/190C. Until the potatoes are cooked and golden brown on top. Garnish with parsley.

   Serves 4.

Chilli Con Carne

1 lb	(454g)	Minced beef	2 tblspns	Oil
2		Red onions, sliced	2 tspns	Chilli powder
1		Green pepper, chopped	1 tspn	Salt
1 x 28oz	(780g)	Tin tomatoes	1/8 tspn	Cayenne pepper
1 x 8oz	(227g)	Canned cream of tomato soup	1/8 tspn	Paprika pepper
1 x 15oz	(420g)	Can red kidney beans, drained		

1. Heat the oil in a saucepan and fry the vegetables until browned, remove from the pan and keep warm.
2. Add the meat to the pan and fry until browned. Return the vegetables to the pan.
3. Add the spices and cook gently for 2 minutes.
4. Add the can of tomatoes and tomato soup. Bring to the boil.
5. Reduce the heat, cover and simmer for 2 hours, stirring occasionally.
6. Add the kidney beans and heat through.
7. Serve with plain boiled rice.

N.B. This improves if left overnight and reheated.

Serves 4/6.

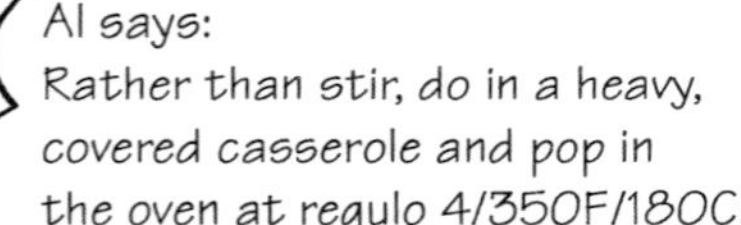

Herby Meat Loaf

8oz	(227g)	Minced Beef
4oz	(113g)	Beef Sausage Meat
1		Egg, beaten
1½oz	(42g)	Bread crumbs
1 tspn		Mixed Herbs

1. Place all of the ingredients into a large bowl, mix well.
2. Place mixture in a greased 1lb loaf tin and cover with foil.
3. Stand the loaf tin in a baking tray filled with water.
4. Bake in the oven for 1½ hours at gas mark 4/180C/375F.
5. Serve with tomato sauce (see next recipe).

Serves 4.

"These cook for a bit longer so go for a wander".

Tomato Sauce

1oz	(30g)	Diced bacon	Garlic, crushed
1oz	(30g)	Diced carrots	Bouquet garni
1oz	(30g)	Diced onions	Salt & pepper
½oz	(15g)	Diced celery	
1 tbspn		Oil	
1oz	(30g)	Plain flour	
1oz	(30g)	Tomato puree	
1pt	(500ml)	Stock (or water and chicken stock cube)	
1 dessertspoon		Vinegar	

1. Heat the oil in a saucepan and fry the bacon, onion, carrot and celery until lightly browned.

2. Add the flour, mix to a smooth paste and cook until lightly brown.

3. Add the tomato puree and mix well. Gradually stir in the boiling stock.

4. Add the garlic, bouquet garni and seasoning. Cover and simmer very gently for 1½ hours.

5. Pass through a strainer or sieve, into a clean pan.

6. Add the vinegar and bring back to the boil.

7. Serve with Herby Meatloaf.

Serves 4.

"These cook for a bit longer so go for a wander".

Hunting Stew

2lb (900g)	Stewing beef (cut into 1" (2cm) cubes)
3	Carrots (chopped)
2	Onions (sliced)
1½ cups	Celery (chopped)
14oz (440g)	Tin chopped tomatoes
1 tblspn	Sugar
3 tblspns	Tapioca
1 tblspn	Lemon Juice
1 tblspn	Worcester sauce
1 tspn	Salt
	Pepper to taste
3-4 cups	Soft white bread crumbs

1. Preheat the oven to gas mark ½/250F/130C.

2. Mix all the ingredients well and put into a 6 pint (3.5ltr) heavy casserole. Cover tightly.

3. Bake for 5 hours DO NOT OPEN THE CASSEROLE!

4. When the stew is cooked add some precooked or canned potatoes and return to the oven until potatoes are heated through.

   Serves 6.

"These cook for a bit longer so go for a wander".

Leave It Alone Pork

6		Small pork chops
2		Pigs kidneys sliced
1 lb	(454g)	Onions, sliced
1½ lb	(680g)	Potatoes, sliced
1 small		Apple chopped
1 tspn		Dried sage
1 tblspn		Tomato sauce

1. Layer the potatoes, onions, apples, pork chops and sliced kidneys in a stew jar or deep casserole, seasoning between layers. Finish with a layer of potatoes.

2. Pour over a teacup of water and cover with a very tight fitting lid.

3. Cook slowly at gas mark 3/325F/160C for at least 2-3 hours.

Serves 6.

"These cook for a bit longer so go for a wander".

Liver Casserole

1 lb	(454g)	Pigs liver, thinly sliced
1 lge		Onion, chopped
2 lbs		Potatoes
6 fl oz	(170ml)	Water and beef stock cube
1 dessertspoon		Dried sage or marjoram or thyme
		Salt & pepper
		Seasoned flour

1. Par-boil and slice the potatoes.

2. Coat the liver with seasoned flour. Place in an ovenproof dish.

3. Add the onions, herbs and seasoning.

4. Pour the stock over the liver, top with sliced potatoes.

5. Cook in the oven for 1½ hours at gas mark 4/180C/350F.

   Serves 4.

Paupers Pork

1lb	(450g)	Lean belly pork, skinned and diced
1lb	(450g)	Potatoes, thinly sliced
1		Onion, chopped
1		Cooking apple, peeled and chopped
5 tblspn		Water
½ tspn		Dried sage
1oz		Butter
		Oil
		Salt and pepper

1. Fry the onion until golden brown. Remove from the pan and place in an oven proof casserole.
2. Fry the pork until brown on all sides. Place in the casserole.
3. Add the apple, seasoning, herbs and water.
4. Overlap the sliced potatoes on top of the pork and dot withbutter.
5. Place in the oven and cook for 1½ hours gas mark 4/350F/180C.

Serves 4.

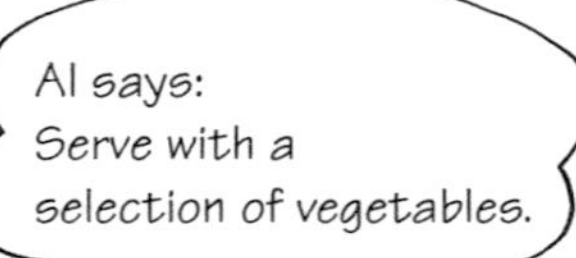

"These cook for a bit longer so go for a wander".

Piquant Pork

4		Lean pork chops
1 oz	(28g)	Margarine or butter
14oz	(400g)	Can chopped tomatoes
1 lge		Onion, peeled and chopped
1		Chicken stock cube dissolved in 1/3rd pt. (200ml) hot water
2 tblspn		Flour
1 tblspn		Tomato puree
1 tblspn		Capers
1 tblspn		Caper liquid
		Salt and pepper
2-3		Sprigs fresh parsley

1. Season the pork with salt and pepper.

2. Melt the margarine or butter in a pan and brown the pork all over. Transfer to a casserole.

3. Brown the onion in the same pan then stir in the flour and cook for 1 minute.

4. Add the chicken stock, tomato puree, salt and pepper, capers and caper liquor. Bring to the boil.

5. Pour over the pork, cover and cook in a moderate oven gas mark 4/350F/180C for 1½ hours until tender.

Serves 4.

Pork and Tomato Casserole

4		Pork chops
14oz	(400g)	Tin chopped tomatoes
2 lge		Onions, sliced
3oz	(85g)	Long grain rice
½ pt	(280ml)	Stock (or water and stock cube)
1oz	(28g)	Butter or cooking oil

1. Heat the oil or butter in a frying pan and gently fry the onions until soft. Put half the onions into a straight sided 2-3 pint (1-1½ ltr) casserole.

2. Scatter half the rice over the onions and top with half the tomatoes.

3. Add the remaining ingredients in similar layers.

4. Place the pork chops on the top, and season.

5. Pour over the stock and cover with a tight fitting lid.

6. Cook in the bottom of the oven for 2½ hours at gas mark 3/325F/160C.

Serves 4.

"These cook for a bit longer so go for a wander".

Pot Roast

3-4 lb	(1.4-1.85kg)	Pot Roast of beef (top side)
1 pkt		Onion soup mix
4¼ fl oz	(120ml)	Red wine or apple juice
		Garlic powder or crushed garlic to taste
¼ tspn		Thyme
		Sugar

1. Line a casserole with two layers of tin foil.

2. Place the meat into centre of the foil and sprinkle with the onion soup mix.

3. Add the red wine (or apple juice) ¼ tspn thyme, garlic powder to taste and a pinch of sugar.

4. Seal the meat in the foil.

5. Cook in the oven for 3 hours at gas mark 3/160C/325F.

   N.B. If you are not ready to eat after 3 hours turn the heat off and allow the meat to rest in the oven; it will remain hot a long time.

   Serves 6/8.

Al says:
If you don't have an oven, use a metal casserole and cook on top of the range using a heat diffuser for 3/5 hours.

Tatie Pot

1 lb	(454g)	Potatoes
1 lb	(454g)	Neck of lamb
8oz	(227g)	Black pudding
1 lge		Onion
½ pt	(280ml)	Stock (water and 2 stock cubes)
		Salt & pepper

1. Peel and slice the potatoes and onion.

2. Cube the lamb and black pudding.

3. Layer the potatoes, black pudding, onions and meat in a deep straight sided casserole, seasoning each layer. Finish with a layer of potatoes.

4. Pour over the hot stock.

5. Cover and bake at gas mark 5/375F/190C for 1½ hours. If black pudding has produced a lot of fat, absorb with crumpled kitchen roll.

6. Remove the lid and cook for a further ½ hour at gas mark 6/400F/200C to brown the potatoes.

Serves 4.

"These cook for a bit longer so go for a wander".

Warming Winter Soup

2 lge	Onions, sliced	2-3oz	Dripping or lard
1 lge	Parsnip, grated	2-3oz	Grated cheese
1 lge	Carrot, grated	1 cup	Pearl barley
15oz (420g)	Tinned chopped tomatoes	1 cup	Red lentils
3	Stock cubes (chicken or beef)		Salt & pepper
2-3	Good pinches mixed herbs		Day old bread
1½ pt (850ml)	Water		
1 dessertspoon	Sugar		

1. In an ovenproof casserole melt the dripping.

2. Put in the sliced onion, grated carrot and parsnip, barley and lentils, mix around in the fat.

3. Add the tomatoes, sugar, herbs, pepper and salt.

4. Add the stock water and stock cubes. Mix everything around well in the casserole.

5. Cover and cook in the oven for 2½ - 3 hours at gas mark 3-4/325-350F/160-180C.

6. Take out the cooked soup.

7. Take the day old bread, slice thickly and remove the crusts. Cut the slices into quarters and place onto top of the soup, press down slightly to soak up some of the liquid.

8. Sprinkle the grated cheese over the top and put under a preheated grill for about 3 minutes until golden brown and bubbling.

Serves 4/6.

4

Easy Cakes That Travel Well

Apple Scone
Apple Cake
Belgian Fruit Loaf
Boiled Fruit Cake
Bran Loaf
Carrot Bread
Canadian Carrot Cake
Caravan Fruit Cake
Chewy Cake
Date and Walnut Cake
Easy Spiced Fruit Loaf
Mincemeat Cake
Peanut Cookies
Tea Time Finger Cakes
Tomato Soup Cake
Weetabix Cake

Apple Scone

6oz	(170g)	Self Raising flour
6oz	(170g)	Cooking apples (weight when peeled and cored)
3oz	(85g)	Margarine
3oz	(85g)	Sugar
		Milk

1. Rub the fat into the flour.

2. Add the diced apple and sugar.

3. Bind together with a little milk into a very firm dough.

4. Roll out to a 7 or 8 inch (17-20cm) round. (Or if the dough is too wet gently press out the dough into a round.) Mark out into sections.

5. Place on a greased baking sheet and bake for 20 minutes at gas mark 5/190C/375F.

6. Reduce the heat and bake for a further 20-25 minutes at gas mark 3/160C/325F.

7. Split open and butter well and eat hot.

Apple Cake

6oz	(170g)	Caster sugar
3oz	(84g)	Butter
8oz	(227g)	Self Raising flour
1oz	(28g)	Candied peel, chopped
1 lb	(454g)	Bramley apples, peeled, cored and diced
2		Eggs, beaten
2 tblspns		Milk
1 tblspn		Granulated sugar
1		Orange rind, grated

1. Line and grease a 9 inch (23cm) cake tin.
2. Cream the butter, sugar and orange rind and beat until light and creamy.
3. Mix 1 tblspn of flour with the apples.
4. Add the eggs and milk.
5. Add the remaining ingredients, except granulated sugar, and mix well.
6. Turn out into the prepared cake tin and sprinkle the top with granulated sugar.
7. Bake for 45-50 minutes at gas mark 4/180C/350F until golden brown.

Belgian Fruit Loaf

2 cups	Milk
2 cups	Sugar
2 cups	Raisins or sultanas
½ lb (225g)	Margarine
1 lb	Self Raising flour
½ -1 tspn	Bicarbonate of soda
2	Eggs

1. Place milk, sugar, fruit and margarine into a large saucepan and bring to the boil stirring occasionally.

2. Allow to cool. Then mix in the flour and bicarbonate of soda.

3. Add the beaten eggs.

4. Divide the mixture between 2 x 2lb (lkg) loaf tins.

5. Bake for 1½ hours at gas mark 3/325F/160C.

Boiled Fruit Cake

8oz	(227g)	Self Raising flour
4oz	(113g)	Margarine or butter
4oz	(113g)	Sugar
12oz	(340g)	Mixed fruit
1		Beaten egg
5 floz	(142ml)	Water

1. Place the margarine or butter, fruit, sugar and water into a pan.

2. Simmer slowly for 20 minutes.

3. Allow to cool.

4. Add the beaten egg to the mixture.

5. Stir in the flour.

6. Pour into a lined and greased 6" cake tin.

7. Bake for 1½ hours at gas mark 2-3: 300-325F or 150-160C.

8. When cooked remove from the tin and cool on a wire rack.

Bran Loaf

4oz	(113g)	All Bran
10oz	(283g)	Mixed dried fruit
10 floz	(284ml)	Milk
5oz	(140g)	Caster sugar
4oz	(113g)	Self Raising flour

1. Put bran, fruit and sugar in a basin.
2. Add the milk and leave to stand for 30 minutes.
3. Mix in the flour.
4. Pour into a lined 2lb loaf tin.
5. Bake for 1 hour at gas mark 4/350F or 180C.
6. When cooked allow to cool in the tin before turning out.

N.B. If you have no sugar, mix ½ pint mug each of All Bran, milk and flour, and 2 x ½ pint mugs of mixed fruit, and follow the method as given above.

Carrot Bread

8oz	(225g)	Sugar
12oz	(340g)	Self Raising flour
1 tspn		Bicarbonate of soda
1 tspn		Mixed spice (or cinnamon)
13oz	(368g)	Can crushed pineapple
6 fl oz	(170ml)	Vegetable oil
2 tspn s		Vanilla essence
1 tspn		Salt
2oz	(50g)	Grated carrot
2oz	(50g)	Chopped nuts

1. Sift together flour, bicarbonate of soda, salt and mixed spice.
2. Mix in the sugar and vegetable oil and vanilla essence.
3. Fold in the grated carrot and the drained crushed pineapple.
4. Add the chopped nuts (optional)
5. Line 3 x 1lb loaf tins. Divide the mixture between the 3 tins.
6. Bake for 50 minutes at gas mark 4/350F/180C.
7. When cooked allow to cool on a wire rack. When cold, wrap in grease proof paper.

Canadian Carrot Cake

4oz	(113g)	Caster sugar
3oz	(85g)	Self Raising flour
		Salt
½ tspn		Ground cinnamon
½ tspn		Bi-carbonate of soda
2 floz	(28ml)	Sunflower oil
1		Egg
3oz	(85g)	Grated carrots
4oz	(113g)	Cream cheese
2oz	(56g)	Butter
2oz	(56g)	Icing sugar
		Vanilla extract
		Chopped nuts

1. Beat the oil and egg into the flour, add sugar, salt, cinnamon and bicarbonate of soda.

2. Add the carrots and mix well.

3. Spread the mixture evenly into a greased and lined 7 inch (17cm) square cake tin.

4. Bake for 45 minutes or until firm at gas mark 4/180C/350F.

5. Cool and split in half when cold.

6. Cream together the cream cheese, butter, icing sugar and vanilla extract.

7. Sandwich the cake together with half the cheese mixture. Top with the remaining mixture and sprinkle with chopped nuts.

Caravan Fruit Cake

12oz	(340g)	Plain flour	2½oz	(70g)	Margarine
6oz	(170g)	Soft brown sugar	6oz	(170g)	Currants
6oz	(170g)	Sultanas	5oz	(140g)	Raisins
1oz	(28g)	Candied peel	2oz	(56g)	Chopped cherries
½ tspn		Mixed Spice	¼ tspn		Cinnamon
¼ tspn		Nutmeg	1 level tspn		Bicarbonate of soda
½ pt	(280ml)	Milk			Pinch of salt

1. Sift together the flour, salt and spices.
2. Rub in the margarine and sugar.
3. Add the fruit and candied peel.
4. Make a well in the centre and add all but 2 tblspns of the milk and mix lightly.
5. Heat the retained milk to blood heat and pour onto the bicarbonate of soda. Then stir into the mixture and mix thoroughly.
6. Place mixture into a greased and lined 7 inch (17cm) square tin.
7. Bake for 1 hour at gas mark 4/350F or 180C. After 1 hour reduce temperature to gas mark 3/325F or 160C and cook for a further hour.

Chewy Cake

4oz (115g) Margarine
8oz (225g) Sugar
8oz (225g) Self Raising flour
8oz (225g) Mixed fruit
2 Eggs
4 tblspns Milk

1. Melt the margarine and pour into a mixing bowl.

2. Stir in the sugar.

3. Beat in the eggs, flour and fruit.

4. Stir in the milk. Grease and line an 8" square, shallow tin. Put mixture into the tin.

5. Bake for 30 minutes at gas mark 3/160C/325F.

Date and Walnut Loaf

8oz	(225g)	Self raising flour
8oz	(225g)	Chopped dates
2oz	(56g)	Chopped walnuts
4oz	(113g)	Vanilla sugar (ordinary sugar may be used but add 1 tspn of Vanilla essence as directed below)
2oz	(56g)	Margarine
6 floz	(170ml)	Water
1 level tspn		Bicarbonate of soda
		Pinch of salt
1		Beaten egg
1 tspn		Vanilla essence (If vanilla sugar is not used)

1. Place the dates, sugar, salt, soda and chopped margarine into a mixing bowl.
2. Boil the water and pour over the ingredients in the mixing bowl, mix well to melt the margarine.
3. Add the beaten egg, walnuts, and flour (and the vanilla essence if used) and mix to a smooth batter type consistency.
4. Pour the mixture into a greased and lined 2lb loaf tin.
5. Bake in the centre of a moderate oven gas mark 3/160C/325F for 1¼ hours until firm.
6. Allow to cool in the tin for 10-15 minutes.

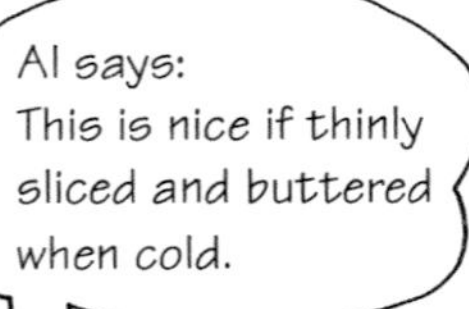

Easy Spiced Fruit Loaf

8oz	(225g)	Self raising flour
4oz	(113g)	Sugar
5 floz	(142ml)	Milk
1 level tspn		Nutmeg
2oz	(56g)	Lard
8oz	(225g)	Mixed dried fruit
1		Egg
1 level tspn		Cinnamon

1. Rub the lard into the flour.
2. Add the rest of the dry ingredients.
3. Beat together the egg and milk and add to the dry ingredients.
4. Pour into a lined 2lb loaf tin.
5. Bake for ¾ hour at gas mark 5/375F or 190C.
6. When cooked turn out and place on a wire rack to cool.

Mincemeat Cake

5oz	(140g)	Soft margarine
8oz	(227g)	Self Raising flour
3		Eggs
		Flaked almonds (optional)
5oz	(140g)	Caster or brown sugar
3oz	(85g)	Sultanas
1lb	(450g)	Jar mincemeat

1. Cream together the margarine and sugar.

2. Add the eggs.

3. Mix in the rest of the ingredients.

4. Pour into a lined and greased 7½ or 8 inch round cake tin.

5. Top with a few flaked almonds.

6. Bake 7½ inch for 1¾ hours or 8 inch cake for 2 hours at gas mark 3/325F or 160C.

7. When cooked remove from the tin and place on a wire rack to cool.

Peanut Cookies

2oz	(56g)	Margarine
2½oz	(70g)	Self Raising flour
2oz	(56g)	Sugar
2oz	(56g)	Salted peanuts

1. Cream the margarine and sugar.
2. Add the flour and nuts mix well.
3. Form into small balls and place well apart on a greased baking sheet, press the tops down slightly.
4. Bake for 15 minutes at gas mark 3-4/325-350F/160-180C.
5. When cooked remove from the baking sheet and place on a wire rack to cool.

Tea Time Finger Cakes

4oz	(113g)	Margarine or butter
6oz	(170g)	Self raising flour
4oz	(113g)	Well chopped nuts
2		Eggs
5oz	(140g)	Demerara sugar
2oz	(56g)	Sultanas
4oz	(113g)	Polka dots (or plain chocolate chips)
½ tspn		Vanilla essence

1. Cream together the sugar and margarine or butter.

2. Add the eggs and beat well.

3. Stir in the remaining ingredients and mix well.

4. Turn into a greased 11 x 7 inch (27 x 17cm) shallow tin.

5. Bake for 40 minutes at gas mark 4/350F or 180C.

6. Leave in tin until cold, then cut into fingers.

Tomato Soup Cake

14oz	(396g)	Plain flour
8oz	(227g)	Soft brown sugar
4oz	(113g)	Butter or margarine
5 level tspns		Baking powder
1 level tspn		Bicarbonate of soda
1½ level tspn		Ground cinnamon
1½ level tspn		Ground nutmeg
½ level tspn		Ground cloves
1 can	(10½oz)	Condensed tomato soup
¼ pt	(142ml)	Water
6oz	(169g)	Raisins
2oz	(113g)	Walnuts or mixed nuts

1. Grease and line a 9" square cake tin.
2. Cream the sugar and butter until light and fluffy.
3. Sift together the flour, baking powder, bicarbonate of soda, and spices.
4. Add the dry ingredients alternately with the soup and water to the creamed mixture.
5. Lightly stir in the raisins and chopped nuts.
6. Turn the mixture into the prepared tin and bake for 1¼ - 1½ hours at gas mark 4/180C/350F.
7. When cooked remove from the tin and remove paper. Leave to cool on a wire rack.

Weetabix Cake

1 cup	Sugar
1 cup	Mixed fruit
1 cup	Milk
2	Weetabix
2 cups	Self raising flour
½ tspn	Mixed spice

1. Put the Weetabix into a bowl and add the milk.

2. Add the remaining ingredients and mix well.

3. Place into a greased and lined 1lb loaf tin.

4. Bake for 1 hour at gas mark 4/180C/350F.

5. Serve cut into thin slices and buttered.

5

Some Favourite Recipes Savoury and Sweet

Beef Stroganoff
Rich Beef Stew
Frog in a Bog
Bombay Salad
Chicken Maryland
Corn Fritters
Chicken Pot Pie
Coq-au-Vin
Coronation Chicken
Fish with Sweetcorn Crumble
Fish Pie
Martinied Meat
Metza Pie
Mock Crab
Mushroom Paté
Sweet Pickled Mushrooms
Pickled Onions in Brown Sugar
Oxtail Casserole
Posh Pork
Raisin Pie
Honeycomb Mould
Impossible Pie
Rich Nut Pie
Raisin Compote
Savoury Christmas Slice

BEEF STROGANOFF

1 lb	(454g)	Beef fillet or rump steak, cut into thin strips
10.4oz	(295g)	Can condensed cream of mushroom soup
¼ pt	(150ml)	Soured cream
1		Onion, finely chopped
1 tblspn		Oil
1 tspn		Tomato puree
		Freshly ground black pepper

1. Heat the oil in a large frying pan and fry the onion for 2 minutes.

2. Add the meat and cook for 5 minutes.

3. Add the remaining ingredients, except soured cream, stir well.

4. Cook for 5 minutes then swirl in the soured cream and serve.

Serves 4.

Rich Beef Stew

1lb	(454g)	Stewing steak	1 glass	Red wine
2oz	(56g)	Button mushrooms	1 tblspn	Tomato puree
1 small		Onion, rough chopped	2	Cloves garlic, crushed
1		Carrot, rough chopped		
1oz	(28g)	Beef dripping (or oil)	1	Bouquet garni
1oz	(28g)	Plain flour	1 tblspn	Fresh chopped parsley
1½ pt	(850ml)	Beef stock (or water and 4 stock cubes)		Salt and freshly ground black pepper

1. Remove any excess fat and sinew from the meat. Cut into 1 inch (2cm) cubes.
2. Heat the dripping in a large saucepan until very hot and quickly fry the meat until lightly browned.
3. Add the roughly chopped vegetables, button mushrooms and garlic. Cook until browned.
4. Add the flour and mix well in, cook until the flour has coloured slightly.
5. Mix in the tomato puree.
6. Add the stock and red wine and bring to the boil, skim off any excess oil or scum.
7. Add the bouquet garni and seasoning.
8. Reduce the heat and cover the pan, simmer until cooked, about 1½ hours.
9. Remove from the sauce and place in a warm serving dish.
10. Correct the consistency and seasoning of the sauce and strain onto the meat.
11. Sprinkle with the chopped parsley and serve.

Serves 4.

Frog in a Bog

FILLING

6oz (170g)	Finely minced beef	1 small	Onion finely chopped
10½oz can	Condensed Tomato or Oxtail Soup	2 tblspns	Curried fruit chutney (optional)
4 level tblspns	Plain flour	1oz (28g)	Butter or oil
½ level tspn	Salt		Pepper

BATTER

2oz (56g)	Dripping	1	Egg
3oz (85g)	Plain flour		Salt & Pepper
¼ pt (142ml)	Milk & water		

1. Put ½ tspn of dripping in each of 16 bun tins. Place in a pre-heated oven gas mark 8/230C/450F.
2. Sift the flour and seasoning into a small bowl.
3. Break in the egg and beat to a smooth thin batter, gradually adding the water and milk.
4. Melt the butter in a pan and gently fry the onion until softened, remove from the pan onto a paper kitchen towel to drain and cool.
5. Mix the beef with half the soup, seasoning, flour, cooked onion and chutney to a thick paste. Form into 16 balls.
6. Place a meat ball in each of the 16 hot smoking tins. Pour batter over each meat ball.
7. Put in the oven and bake for 15 minutes, until well risen and crisp and golden.
8. Heat the remaining soup and serve as a sauce.

Serves 4.

Al says:
You've heard of Toad in a Hole....?
Well!?!?!!

Bombay Salad

1 tin	Corned beef (chilled and finely diced)
1 tin	Pineapple chunks, drained
1 tblspn	Dessicated coconut
1 tblspn	Raisins
1 level tspn	Curry powder
4 tblspns	Salad cream (not mayonnaise)

Combine all ingredients together and serve with a green salad.

Serves 4.

Chicken Maryland

4 lb	(1.8kg)	Chicken joints	
1½oz	(40g)	Plain flour	
½oz	(15g)	Salt	
1 tspn		Paprika pepper	
1 tspn		Freshly ground black pepper	
		Pinch Cayenne pepper	
2		Eggs)	beaten together
3 tblspns		Milk)	
5 floz	(142ml)	Cooking oil	

1. Mix the spices and seasoning with the flour.

2. Coat the chicken pieces with the seasoned flour, dip into the beaten egg and milk, then again in the seasoned flour.

3. Heat the oil in a large frying pan, start by frying the dark meat first, add the white meat 5 minutes later.

4. Turn the pieces once during frying, allowing 20 minutes for the dark meat and 15 minutes for the white meat.

5. Drain onto kitchen paper and serve with corn fritters (see next recipe!).

   Serves 4.

CORN FRITTERS

8oz	(225g)	Frozen corn kernels (defrosted)
4 tblspns		Double cream
2 tblspns		Plain flour
½ tspn		Baking powder
½ tspn		Sugar
		Salt and freshly ground black pepper

1. Place all of the ingredients into a mixing bowl and beat well.

2. Heat a large frying pan and grease it lightly with a small knob of butter.

3. Drop spoonfuls of the mixture into it, flatten them slightly with a palette knife.

4. Cook until golden brown on each side.

Serves 4.

Chicken Pot Pie

1 lge		Chicken
2		Green peppers
1 stick		Celery
8oz	(227g)	Onion, chopped
4oz	(113g)	Button mushrooms
2oz	(56g)	Butter
1oz	(28g)	Flour
1 pt	(568ml)	Chicken stock
½ pt	(284ml)	Milk
1 pkt		Frozen puff pastry
		Dried sage
		Dried parsley
		Salt & pepper

1. Boil the chicken until cooked and retain the cooking liquor. Return the liquor to the pan and reduce to 1 pint.
2. Strip the meat from the chicken carcass, discard the carcass and break the meat into pieces and put aside.
3. Melt the butter in a saucepan, add the onions, celery and peppers, cook gently until tender.
4. Stir in the flour and cook gently for a few minutes. Add the stock and milk, bring to the boil stirring until the sauce thickens.
5. Add the mushrooms and cooked chicken to the sauce and heat through.
6. Correct the seasoning and pour into a pie dish.

either

7a. Roll out the pastry and cut into rectangles and bake on a greased baking sheet.

or

7b. Put a pie funnel in the pie dish, then roll out the pastry and cover the pie dish, making a steam hole for the funnel.

8. For either version bake everything for 15-20 minutes at gas mark 7/220C/425F.

Serves 4.

Coq-Au-Vin

1oz	(25g)	Margarine or butter
4oz	(113g)	Streaky bacon (diced)
4oz	(113g)	Button mushrooms
4		Chicken joints
12		Button onions (whole) or shallots
1		Clove garlic (crushed)
2 tblspns		Tomato puree
1/3 pt	(200ml)	Chicken stock (or water and a stock cube)
8 fl oz	(225ml)	Red wine
		Pinch of thyme
1		Bay leaf
		Salt & black pepper
1 tblspn		Cornflour

1. Melt the margarine or butter and saute the chicken joints until golden brown, remove from the pan and place in a casserole.
2. Fry the onions, bacon and garlic until golden brown. Add to the chicken.
3. Blend the tomato puree with the stock (or water and a stock cube) and pour over the chicken. Add the red wine.
4. Add the herbs, seasoning and mushrooms and cover the casserole.
5. Bake in the centre of the oven for 1½ hours at gas mark 4/350F/180C.
6. Remove from the oven and skim off any excess fat.
7. Mix the cornflour with a little cold water and add to the mixture.
8. Return to the oven and cook for a further 15-20 minutes.
9. Before serving remove the bay leaf.

Serves 4.

Coronation Chicken

1 lge		Chicken, cooked and cut into bite sized pieces	2 tbspns		Lemon Juice
			5 floz	(142ml)	Red wine
2 lge		Onion, chopped	2 cups		Brown rice or long grain and wild rice
1 Jar	(14oz)	Mayonnaise			
5oz	(140g)	Natural Yoghurt	3oz	(84g)	Sultanas
2oz	(56g)	Butter	3oz	(84g)	Dried apricots
1 dessertspoon		Curry paste	3 tblspns		Olive oil
1 tbspn		Tomato paste	3 tblspns		Wine vinegar
2 tbspns		Apricot Jam	2oz	(56g)	Butter

1. Bring 4 cups of water to the boil in a saucepan add the rice and cook until almost tender.
2. Add the sultanas and dried apricots and continue cooking until the rice is cooked and all of the water absorbed, drain.
3. Add the olive oil and wine vinegar.
4. Meanwhile melt the butter in a frying pan and fry the onions until lightly browned.
5. Add the curry paste and stir well.
6. Mix in the tomato paste, red wine and lemon juice, stir well to prevent sticking.
7. Remove from the heat and add the yoghurt, jam and mayonnaise.
8. Return to a low heat and add the chicken pieces, cook gently until the chicken is heated through.

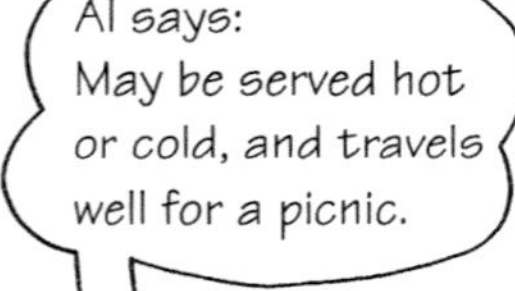

Serves 6.

Fish with Sweetcorn Crumble

SAUCE			FISH	
1oz	(28g)	Margarine or butter	4	Fillets of Sole or Plaice
1oz	(28g)	Flour	1	Egg
½ pt	(284ml)	Milk	3oz (85g)	Golden breadcrumbs
7oz	(198g)	Can of sweetcorn drained	2	Stock cubes
			1 tblspn	Plain flour
2		Eggs		Salt & pepper
8oz	(227g)	Cottage cheese		
		Salt & pepper		
6		Cloves		
2		Bayleaves		
1 small		Onion		
CRUMBLE				
4oz	(113g)	Plain flour		
2oz	(56g)	Butter		

1. Stud a small onion with a bayleaf and 2 cloves, place in the milk and bring almost to boiling point. Remove the studded onion.
2. Melt 1oz butter in a saucepan, stir in 1oz of flour and cook gently.
3. Whisk in the milk and bring to the boil and stir until the sauce thickens.
4. Add the drained sweetcorn, beaten egg and cottage cheese.
5. Rub 2oz of butter into 4oz plain flour (so that it resembles coarse breadcrumbs).
6. Pour the sauce into an ovenproof casserole and top with the crumble mixture.
7. Bake for 50 minutes at gas mark 5/190C/375F until golden brown.
8. Put 1 tblspn of flour seasoned with salt and pepper in a plastic bag.
9. Beat the egg in a bowl.
10. Put the breadcrumbs and crumbled stock cubes onto a plate.
11. Cut the fish into strips and place in the plastic bag with the flour and shake vigourously until the fish is coated with flour.
12. Remove the fish from the bag and dip in the beaten egg.
13. Coat with the breadcrumbs.
14. Fry in deep oil for 3 minutes until golden brown.

Fish Pie

1½ lbs	(680g)	White Fish
4oz	(113g)	Cooked shelled prawns (optional)
2lbs	(908g)	Cooked potatoes
1 pt	(568ml)	Milk
6oz	(169g)	Butter
2oz	(56g)	Plain flour
3		Eggs, hard boiled and chopped
2 tblspns		Tartare sauce
		Fresh parsley, chopped
		Salt & pepper
2oz		Cheddar cheese, grated

1. Gently poach the fish in ½ pt (280ml) milk.
2. Drain the fish and reserve the milk.
3. Skin and break the fish into flakes.
4. Place the eggs, fish and prawns (optional) into an ovenproof dish.
5. Melt the butter in a saucepan and stir in the flour. Cook until all the flour is absorbed.
6. Whisk in the reserved cooking liquid and remaining milk, bring to the boil whisking all the time until the sauce thickens.
7. Stir in the tartare sauce, parsley and seasonings.
8. Add to the fish in the casserole.
9. Mash the potatoes with 2oz (56g) butter and a little milk.
10. Spoon or pipe over the fish to cover the casserole.
11. Bake for ½-¾ hour at gas mark 6/200C/400F.
12. Top with grated cheese and pop under the grill.

Serves 4.

Martinied Meat

1lb (454g)	Pork escalope (or chicken or veal) flattened and cut into pieces
	Seasoned flour
2oz (56g)	Butter
4 tblspns	Dry Martini
4 tblspns	Fresh beef stock
8	Spring onions, chopped
1 dessertspoon	Fresh chopped parsley
	Sprigs of fresh rosemary
1	Lemon, thinly sliced

1. Coat the meat in seasoned flour.

2. Melt the butter in a frying pan and quickly fry the meat until browned.

3. Add the Martini and stock, bring to the boil and cook for 5 minutes until the liquid has reduced and thickened.

4. Add the rosemary, chopped parsley, spring onions and sliced lemon.

5. Simmer for 2-3 minutes and serve.

Serves 4.

Metza Pie

Imperial	Metric	Ingredient
1lb	(454g)	Minced beef
3oz	(84g)	Dry breadcrumbs
4 fl oz	(113ml)	Milk
2 tspns		Onion salt
4 tblspns		Tomato ketchup
2 tspns		Dried Oregano
4oz	(113g)	Sliced mushrooms
4oz	(113g)	Grated cheddar cheese

1. Pre-heat the oven to gas mark 5/190C/375F.
2. Mix together the minced beef, breadcrumbs, milk and onion salt.
3. Mould the mixture onto a 9 inch (23cm) ovenproof pie plate to form a shell.
4. Spread with the tomato ketchup and sprinkle with oregano.
5. Top with the mushrooms and cover with grated cheese.
6. Bake for 35 minutes.
7. Cut into four portions.

Serves 4.

Al says:
Serve with a salad and french bread. This is pizza with mince instead of pastry.

Mock Crab

4		Ripe Skinned Tomatoes
3oz	(85g)	Grated Cheddar Cheese
1oz	(28g)	Butter
1		Egg
		Salt & pepper
		Melted butter to preserve

1. Place the tomatoes in a saucepan and beat to a pulp.
2. Add the butter and cook for a few minutes.
3. Add the cheese and seasoning.
4. Add the egg and stir until it thickens.
5. Put into jars and cover with melted butter.
6. Spread on toast fingers or use for sandwiches.

Serves 2.

MUSHROOM PATÉ

1 sm		Onion, chopped	7oz	(198g)	Butter
8oz	(227g)	Flat mushrooms	6oz	(169g)	Cream cheese
8oz	(227g)	Button mushrooms	2 tbspns		Mayonnaise
6 fl oz	(170ml)	Red wine	2		Bay leaves
10 fl oz	(284ml)	Aspic jelly, made up and cooled	2		Cloves garlic, crushed

TO GARNISH

Sliced Raw Mushrooms
Lettuce
Lemon slices
Melba toast

1. Heat 4oz butter in a large saucepan and gently fry the onions and garlic for 5 minutes until softened.
2. Add the flat mushrooms, wine and bay leaves. Boil rapidly until reduced by half.
3. Discard the bay leaves. Puree in a processor.
4. Stir in half the aspic jelly.
5. Pour into a loaf tin lined with cling film. Chill until set.
6. Gently fry the button mushrooms in the remaining 3oz butter for 5 minutes.
7. Place in a processor with the remaining aspic, the cream cheese and mayonnaise, blend until smooth.
8. Pour onto the set mixture in the loaf tin, chill until set.
9. When set dip the tin in hot water before turning out. Remove cling film.
10. Garnish with sliced raw mushrooms.
11. Serve, cut in slices with lettuce, melba toast and lemon slices.

Serves 6/8.

Sweet Pickled Mushrooms

1½ lbs	(680g)	Small button mushrooms, sliced
2oz	(56g)	Finely chopped onion
2oz	(56g)	Pickled gerkins, chopped
4 level tblspns		Mango chutney, chopped
1 level tblspn		Chilli seasoning
3 tblspns		White wine vinegar
5 floz	(142ml)	Water
		Salt & pepper

1. Place the mushrooms and onions in a large pan.

2. Add the chopped gerkins, mango chutney and chilli seasoning.

3. Add the water and wine vinegar then bring to the boil.

4. Cover with a tight fitting lid and simmer for 5-10 minutes. DO NOT OVER COOK.

5. Allow to cool then chill.

6. Serve with french bread and salad as a starter or as a seperate cold vegetable dish.

Pickled Onions in Brown Sugar

5lbs	(2.4kg)	Pickling onions
3 pts	(1.7 ltrs)	Malt vinegar
1½ lbs	(680g)	Demerara sugar
1oz	(28g)	Pickling spice

1. Pour boiling water onto the onions and leave until cold.
2. Peel the onions and leave overnight in cold salted water.
3. Boil together the vinegar, spices and sugar.
4. As soon as the vinegar has boiled remove from the heat and allow to go cold.
5. Drain, rinse and dry the onions.
6. Pack into jars, cover with the vinegar and seal the jars.

Oxtail Casserole

1		Oxtail (cut into joints)
2		Beef stock cubes (crumbled into 2 pts (1.13 ltr) hot water)
2		Onions, peeled and sliced
2		Carrots, peeled and sliced
1oz	(28g)	Margarine
1oz	(28g)	Plain flour
4oz	(113g)	Mushrooms
2 tblspns		Tomato puree
		Salt & pepper
1		Bouquet garni
2-3		Sprigs fresh parsley

1. Place the oxtail in a saucepan with the beef stock and bouquet garni.
2. Bring to the boil and simmer gently for 1½ - 2 hours.
3. Strain the liquor and skim off the fat when cold. Make up to 1 pint (575ml) with cold water if necessary.
4. Place the vegetables in a casserole with the oxtails on top.
5. Place the margarine, flour and reserved liquor in a saucepan over a moderate heat.
6. Bring to the boil, whisking continuously. Cook for 2-3 minutes, still whisking until thickened, smooth and glossy.
7. Add seasoning and tomato puree.
8. Pour over the oxtail and cover
9. Bake for 1½ hours at gas mark 3/325F/160C.
10. Add the mushrooms and cook for a further 20-30 minutes.
11. Garnish with chopped parsley.

Serves 4.

Posh Pork

1½ lb	(680g)	Lean pork shoulder, diced
2 med		Onions, sliced
14oz	(400g)	Tin chopped tomatoes
8 floz	(227ml)	Red wine
½ pt	(250ml)	Chicken stock (or water and stock cube)
2oz	(56g)	Stuffed olives, sliced
2oz	(56g)	Black olives
2		Cloves garlic, crushed
2 tblspns		Cooking oil
		Seasoned flour
2 tspns		Dried oregano

1. Heat the oil in a pan and fry the pork until browned.

2. Remove the meat from the pan with a slotted spoon and place in an ovenproof casserole.

3. Add the onions and garlic to the pan and fry until golden brown.

4. Add sufficient flour to absorb the fat and cook until light brown in colour. Allow to cool slightly.

5. Slowly add the stock, red wine and tomatoes stirring all the time.

6. Pour the sauce over the meat in the casserole.

7. Mix in the herbs and seasoning.

8. Place in a pre heated oven gas mark 2/150C/300F for 1½ - 2½ hours.

Serves 4/6.

Raisin Pie

12oz (340g)	Raisins
3oz (85g)	Soft brown sugar
10oz (285g)	Plain flour
1 oz (28g)	Butter
2½oz (70g)	Margarine
2½oz (70g)	Lard
¾ pt (425ml)	Water
¼ pt (142ml)	Orange juice
1 tspn	Grated orange rind
1 level tblspn	Cornflour
1 level tspn	Cinnamon
1 tspn	Vinegar

1. Place ½ pt water and the raisins in a saucepan.
2. Mix the sugar, rind, cinnamon, salt and cornflour in a basin and mix to a smooth paste with a little orange juice.
3. Add the remaining orange juice to the raisins and bring to the boil. Cook gently for 5 minutes.
4. Stir in the blended cornflour and cook for a further 2 minutes.
5. Remove from the heat and stir in the butter and vinegar. Allow to cool.
6. Sieve the flour and salt into a mixing bowl.
7. Rub the fats into the flour until it reaches a sandy texture.
8. Bind together with a little cold water.
9. Place pastry in a plastic bag and put in a fridge for 20 minutes.
10. Roll out ½ the pastry to fit a 9 inch (22cm) pie plate.
11. Place the cooled filling into the case, roll out the remaining pastry to cover the pie.
12. Bake for 30 minutes at gas mark 6/400F/200C.
13. Serve cold, or hot with custard or chilled double cream.

Serves 6/8.

Honeycomb Mould

2		Eggs
2 oz	(56g)	Sugar
½oz	(14g)	Gelatine
1pt	(560ml)	Milk
1 tspn		Vanilla essence

1. Put the egg yolks, sugar, gelatine and a little milk into a saucepan and mix well, add the remaining milk and heat gently stirring all the time.

2. Cook the custard, without boiling, stirring continuously until it thickens slightly.

3. Remove from the heat and stir in the vanilla essence. Set aside until it begins to set.

4. Whisk the egg whites stiffly and fold them through the custard mixture.

5. Turn into a 1 pint mould and leave to set.

Serves 4.

Impossible Pie

4oz (113g)	Butter
8oz (227g)	Caster Sugar
8oz (227g)	Dessicated coconut
4	Eggs
4oz (113g)	Plain flour
½ tspn	Vanilla extract
½ tspn	Ground nutmeg
½ pt (284ml)	Milk

1. Pre-heat the oven to gas mark 4/180C/350F.

2. Lightly grease a 10 inch (25.5cm) pie dish or flan dish.

3. Place all the ingredients in a processor and blend until smooth.

4. Pour into the prepared dish and bake in the oven for 1 hour.

5. Serve this pie hot or cold with cream or custard.

Serves 6/8.

Rich Nut Pie

PASTRY

12oz	(340g)	Plain flour
3oz	(84g)	Lard
5oz	(140g)	Butter
5oz	(140g)	Granulated sugar
1		Egg
1		Beaten egg to glaze

FILLING

8oz	(227g)	Granulated sugar
8 floz	(227ml)	Double cream
8oz	(227g)	Chopped walnuts

A 7" flan ring is required and a baking sheet.

PASTRY

1. Place the flour into a bowl and rub in the butter and lard until it resembles fine bread crumbs.
2. Add the sugar to the mixture.
3. Blend together with an egg and gently knead to a smooth dough. Divide into 2 pieces.
4. Turn onto a lightly floured surface and roll each half to the size of the flan ring plus a 2" rim. Place flan ring onto a greased baking sheet
5. Use one half of the pastry to line the flan ring. Prick the base with a fork and place in the fridge to chill.

FILLING

6. Sprinkle 8oz sugar into a heavy heated frying pan and stir until it caramalises and turns to a golden liquid.
7. Heat the cream, add to the sugar and stir thoroughly, increase the heat for a few moments.
8. Remove the pan from the heat and add the chopped walnuts. Allow to cool slightly.
9. Remove the flan case from the fridge and pour the walnut mixture into it. Then seal with a lid made from the remaining pastry. Glaze with beaten egg. Make a steam hole.
10. Bake in a pre-heated oven gas mark 4/180C/350F for 35 minutes.
11. When cooked cool slightly and remove from the flan ring.

N.B. This pie is rich and goes a long way.

SERVE EITHER HOT OR COLD

Raisin Compote

4oz	(113g)	Californian Raisins
4oz	(113g)	Dried Figs
4oz	(113g)	Dried Apricots
1 pt	(570ml)	Water
1½oz	(42g)	Muscavado Sugar
2 inch		Cinnamon Stick
		Banana chips (optional)

1. Place the dried fruit in a bowl and cover with water. Leave overnight.

2. Drain the liquid into a saucepan and add the sugar and cinnamon.

3. Heat gently until the sugar dissolves. Increase the heat and bring to the boil for 5 minutes.

4. Return the fruit to the pan and simmer for 20 minutes until tender.

5. Serve hot or cold sprinkled with banana chips.

Serves 4.

Savoury Christmas Slice

FILLING				
1lb	(454g)	Minced pork	¼ tspn	Mace
8oz	(227g)	Minced beef	½ tspn	Celery salt
1lb	(454g)	Potatoes, cooked and mashed	¼ tspn	Ground cloves
2 sm		Onions, diced	1	Clove garlic (whole)
6 floz		Water		
¾ tspn		Salt		
¼ tspn		Sage		

PASTRY		
9oz	(255g)	Plain flour
4½oz	(127g)	Lard or margarine
5½ tblspns		Cold water
1 tspn		Salt

1. Sieve the flour and 1 tspn salt into a medium mixing bowl.
2. Rub in the fat so that it resembles fine breadcrumbs.
3. Bind together with 5½ tblspns cold water.
4. Divide into 4 and place in the fridge to rest for 20 minutes.
5. Roll pastry into rounds to line and cover 2 x 7 inch loose bottom flan tins.
6. Place all of the filling ingredients into a heavy pan and bring to the boil.
7. Reduce the heat and cook uncovered for 20 minutes.
8. Remove the clove of garlic. The mixture should be moist but not watery.
9. Cook for another few minutes
10. Pour into the prepared pastry cases and cover with the remaining pastry rounds. Trim the edges and make a steam vent in the centre.
11. Bake for 10 minutes at regulo 8/230C/450F.
12. Reduce the heat to gas mark 4/180C/350F and bake for a further ½ hour until the pastry is golden brown.

Serves 8.

6

A Selection of "No Bake" Cakes and Desserts

Almond Slices
Blackberry Bombe
Chocolate and Date Fingers
Chocolate Oat Crunchies
Chocolate Marsh Mallows
Crispy Coconut Fingers
Oat Squares
Pear and Lime Cream
Chocolate Fridge Cake
Vancouver Bars
White Chocolate Mousse
Raspberry or Blackcurrant Sauce
Tiramisu
Anne's Punch
Sloe Gin

ALMOND SLICES

8oz	(227g)	Condensed milk
8oz	(227g)	Rich tea biscuits, finely crushed
4oz	(113g)	Block margarine
3oz	(85g)	Dessicated coconut
½ tspn		Almond essence

1. Place the margarine and condensed milk in a saucepan and heat gently until melted.

2. Remove from the heat then add the almond essence.

3. Mix the biscuits and coconut together. Add to the melted mixture and mix well.

4. Press into the a greased and lined 7" square tin and leave to set.

Blackberry Bombe

PUREE

1lb	(454g)	Brambles
4oz	(113g)	Sugar
1 tblspn		Water

ICE CREAM

½ pt	(284ml)	Fruit puree
½ pt	(284ml)	Whipping cream
3oz	(85g)	Broken meringue

1. Puree the fruit, sugar and water in a blender or processor.
2. Pass the puree through a fine strainer.
3. Whip the cream into soft peaks.
4. Fold in the meringue.
5. Add ½ pint (284ml) of the puree and ripple it through the cream. DO NOT OVER MIX.
6. Turn into a 2 pint pudding basin and chill well or part freeze.
7. To serve dip the basin in hot water and invert onto a plate.
8. Spoon some of the remaining puree over the bombe.

Serves 6.

Chocolate and Date Fingers

5oz	(140g)	Chopped dates
4oz	(113g)	Block margarine
4oz	(113g)	Caster sugar
3oz	(85g)	Rice krispies
6oz	(170g)	Chocolate
2 tspns		Milk

1. Grease and line a deep 7 x 11 inch (17 x 27cm) tin.

2. Melt the margarine in a saucepan and add the chopped dates and sugar. Stir over a gentle heat until the mix boils and thickens.

3. Remove from the heat and stir in the rice krispies, mix thoroughly.

4. Press mixture into the tin and leave until firm.

5. Melt the chocolate and milk in a double pan, when melted spread over the base and leave to set.

6. Cut into fingers.

Chocolate Oat Crunchies

8oz	(227g)	Chocolate
8oz	(227g)	Crunchy oat cereal
2oz	(56g)	Butter
1½oz	(42g)	Dessicated coconut
2 tblspns		Honey

1. Melt together the chocolate, butter and honey in a double pan.

2. Add the cereal and coconut. Stir well.

3. Spoon into bun cases and leave to set.

Chocolate Marsh Mallows

14oz	(400g)	Tin condensed milk
8oz	(227g)	Caster sugar
4oz	(113g)	Plain flour
1oz	(28g)	Cocoa
4oz	(113g)	Butter
3oz	(85g)	Chopped walnuts
5oz	(140g)	Roughly broken digestive biscuits
6oz	(170g)	Marshmallows, chopped
6oz	(170g)	Melted chocolate
1 tspn		Vanilla extract

1. Put the condensed milk into a saucepan and add the sugar, flour, cocoa and butter.

2. Bring slowly to the boil stirring all the time for 1 minute. Allow to cool slightly.

3. Stir in the nuts, biscuits and vanilla extract.

4. Add the marshmallows and stir lightly to create a marbled effect.

5. Pour into a greased 9 x 12 inch (22x 30cm) square tin.

6. Leave overnight to set.

7. Cut into shapes and dip in melted chocolate, decorate with nuts.

Crispy Coconut Fingers

6oz	(170g)	Marshmallows
6oz	(170g)	Chocolate
3oz	(85g)	Rice krispies
2oz	(56g)	Coconut
1oz	(28g)	Butter

1. Line and grease an 8 inch (20cm) square tin.

2. Melt the marshmallows, chocolate, coconut and butter in a saucepan and mix well. Add rice krispies and stir until well coated.

3. Press into the tin and leave to set.

4. Cut into fingers or squares.

Oat Squares

8oz	(227g)	Granulated Sugar
6oz	(170g)	Chocolate
6oz	(170g)	Porridge Oats
2oz	(56g)	Cocoa
2oz	(56g)	Butter
2oz	(56g)	Peanut Butter
2 floz	(57ml)	Milk
½ tspn		Vanilla extract

1. Place the sugar, cocoa, milk, butter and peanut butter into a saucepan and bring to the boil. Boil for 1 minute.

2. Remove from the heat and add porridge oats and vanilla extract.

3. Press mixture into prepared tin. Mark into squares whilst still warm.

4. Melt the chocolate in a double pan, when melted spread over the base and allow to set.

5. Cut into squares.

Pear and Lime Cream

1 pkt	Lime Jelly
	Hot Water
15oz (424g)	Tinned Pears
1 pkt	Dream Topping
½ cup	Cold Milk

1. Dissolve the jelly in hot water, make up to 1 pint with the syrup from the pears. Leave until almost set.

2. Make up the dream topping with the cold milk as directed on the packet, and whisk into the setting jelly.

3. Chop the pears and stir into the jelly cream, turn into a jelly mould and chill until set firmly.

Chocolate Fridge Cake

8oz	(227g)	Digestive biscuits, crushed
7oz	(200g)	Plain chocolate
4oz	(113g)	Butter
4oz	(113g)	Icing sugar
5 fl oz(142ml)		Double cream
¼ tspn		Vanilla extract

1. Lightly grease a 7 inch (17cm) flan ring.

2. Break 6oz (170g) chocolate into a basin over a pan of hot water or into a double pan. Stir until melted.

3. Cream the butter, add the icing sugar and beat until light and fluffy.

4. Stir in the melted chocolate, biscuits and vanilla extract. Mix well.

5. Turn into prepared flan ring. Place in fridge for at least 1 hour (or overnight) until set.

6. Remove from the tin.

7. Whip the cream until stiff and spread over the crunch cake.

8. Grate 1oz (28g) chocolate over the cream.

Serves 6/8.

Vancouver Bars

12oz	(340g)	Icing Sugar
7oz	(200g)	Block Margarine
6oz	(170g)	Crushed digestive biscuits
2oz	(56g)	Dessicated coconut
2oz	(56g)	Chopped nuts
1½oz	(42g)	Caster sugar
3 tblspns		Cocoa powder
3 tblspns		Hot water
3 tblspns		Custard powder
1 tspn		Vanilla extract
1		Egg

1, Melt 4oz (113g) margarine in a saucepan. Add the caster sugar and cocoa powder. Heat gently until the sugar has dissolved.

2. Add the egg and vanilla extract. Cook for 1 minute but DO NOT BOIL.

3. Stir in the biscuits, coconut and nuts.

4. Press the mixture into a greased 6 x 12 inch (15 x 30cm) tin.

5. Leave overnight in the fridge.

6. Beat together 3oz (84g) margarine, icing sugar, hot water and custard powder.

7. Spread this mixture over the base and chill until set.

8. Cut into fingers.

White Chocolate Mousse

2 lge		Bars white chocolate
6 lge		Eggs, separated
1oz	(28g)	Butter
1 sachet		Gelatine
¼ pt	(142ml)	Double cream

1. Whisk the egg yolks until pale and fluffy.
2. Melt the chocolate and butter in a double pan.
3. Mix the melted chocolate into the egg yolks.
4. Add the dissolved gelatine (follow the instructions on the packet).
5. Whip the cream and fold it into the chocolate.
6. Whisk the egg whites to stiff peaks. Fold into the chocolate mixture using a metal spoon.
7. Pour into a mould and place in the fridge to set.

Serves 6.

Raspberry or Blackcurrant Sauce

10oz (283g)	Frozen berries of your choice
	Juice of 1 lemon
	Sugar to taste

1. Place all the ingredients in a blender or processor and puree.
2. Pass through a fine strainer to remove the seeds.

TIRAMISU

6 floz	(170ml)	Strong Black Coffee
8oz	(225g)	Mascarpone Cheese
2oz	(56g)	Grated Dark Chocolate
10 floz	(284ml)	Double cream lightly whipped
3 tblspns		Brandy
3 tblspns		Marsala wine
8		Trifle sponges

1. Thoroughly stir the cheese and cream together.

2. Mix the cold coffee, wine and brandy together.

3. Arrange 4 trifle sponges in the bottom of a dish, very slowly pour half the coffee mixture over the sponges.

4. Add half the cheese then put remaining trifle sponges on top.

5. Sprinkle over the remaining coffee mix.

6. Cover with the remaining cheese mixture.

7. Top with grated chocolate and chill for at least 2 hours before serving.

Serves 6.

Anne's Punch

2 pt	(1.13 ltr)	Cider
½ pt	(284ml)	Sherry
1 small can		Concentrated orange juice (frozen type)
		Rum to taste
		Slices of orange and lemon
2oz	(56g)	Sugar

1. Mix all the ingredients together and leave for several hours.

2. Warm through before serving and float the slices of fruit on the top.

SLOE GIN

1 Litre	Gin
2 lbs	Sloes
1½ lbs	Sugar

1. Prick the sloes with a bodkin or needle.

2. Put into Demi-john or similar, pour in sugar, then pour over the gin.

3. Insert cork, shake everyday for 7/10 days. Leave in the dark for at least 6 weeks, (preferably 1 year).

4. Sit back and enjoy small shots at regular intervals.

Index